T0278945

# from time to new
## Lydia Kwa

Edited by Shane Neilson
Cover and book design by Jeremy Luke Hill
Proofread by Mary Hamilton
Set in Linux Libertine and CarlMarx
Printed on Coach House Laid
Printed and bound by Arkay Design & Print

LIBRARY AND ARCHIVES CANADA CATALOGUING IN PUBLICATION

Title: From time to new / Lydia Kwa.
Names: Kwa, Lydia, 1959- author.
Identifiers: Canadiana (print) 20240370627 | Canadiana (ebook) 20240370643 |
    ISBN 9781774221501 (softcover) | ISBN 9781774221518 (PDF) |
    ISBN 9781774221525 (EPUB)
Subjects: LCGFT: Poetry.
Classification: LCC PS8571.W3 F76 2024 | DDC C811/.54—dc23

The Porcupine's Quill gratefully acknowledges the support of the Canada Council for the Arts, the Ontario Arts Council, and the Ontario Book Publishing Tax Credit.

The Porcupine's Quill respectfully acknowledges the ancestral homelands of the Attawandaron, Anishinaabe, Haudenosaunee, and Métis Peoples, and recognizes that we are situated on Treaty 3 territory, the traditional territory of Mississaugas of the Credit First Nation.

The Porcupine's Quill also recognizes and supports the diverse persons who make up its community, regardless of race, age, culture, ability, ethnicity, nationality, gender identity and expression, sexual orientation, marital status, religious affiliation, and socioeconomic status.

The Porcupine's Quill
130 Dublin Street North
Guelph, Ontario, Canada
N1H 4N4
www.porcupinesquill.ca

For the tender and vulnerable

# Table of Contents

## distant shore

## mixed ethers

## from time to new

*I left half of my language behind to escape my impeccable persona*

— Mary Jean Chan,
"A Wild Patience Has Taken Me This Far"

# distant shore

# Cloudscapes

1.

pre-dusk phoenixes
with razor sharp wings

pterodactyls of the ether

2.

a dark pink trail
as light disappears

3.

life that asks
to be imagined

4.

if you look up
admit surrender

5.

transported
while on earth

6.

to an imminent
ocean

# Digging for Clams

at five, you approach shoreline as
a salty breeze on your lips
feel of hot sand
between toes

you're shown how to
dig down for *coquina* clams

the tiny shells open
in a Tupperware bowl
of soy sauce

you marvel at
your mother's magic trick
learn instantly
that slaughter is easy

reach in to
lift a splayed bivalve
to your mouth—

bursts of
sweet flesh on your tongue

# Shoreline

sand shipped from Cambodia
extended against ocean
as if land were rightfully ours

in the evenings, walking along
East Coast Park near my mum's flat

it's hard to remember where
the original shoreline was

(where once, a child dug for clams)

sunsets are spectacular:
humans on breakwaters
anonymous
romantic silhouettes

while in the far distance
the squadron of tankers
a constant

ocean's protest
subterranean roil & rumble

ghetto blasters &
charcoal pits
bacchanalia on land

# My Father Sold Pineapples

He was eleven, forced to
eat the pineapples he couldn't sell

In Muar with his brothers
during the occupation

Pineapples on an empty stomach
ruined him for life

His uncle reached for the spanner
and struck his head

Fear and hunger, his daily diet
until he grew up to be a charmer

That hollow in him
restless seeking

# Ode to Tofu

Once misunderstood as boring, but now revered
You've emerged from your peasant roots
To seduce the West by casting off veils
Even Salomé can't compete

Such a flirt you've become
Going from soft to firm to skin
Words like "tempeh" no longer mysterious
But cutting-edge vegan

Have you betrayed your humble origins
By catering to the wealthy and presumptuous?
Or are you well-accomplished in equanimity
A shape-shifting internationalist?

My childhood love,
I confess to lapses
In my devotion, too easily
Waylaid by glittery gourmands

Now I wade through soft, familiar waves
Splashed with savoury mushrooms
Or deep-dive into an ocean of black sesame
To drown my sorrows

When fragrant steam rises from the opened vat
And the tin scoop gleans
Scalloped portions laced with ginger syrup
I fall for your ageless charms

# Dancing Together

in Shanghai 1987
they dance ballroom
on the worn parquet floor

men with men
women with women

keeping distance
while touch seems perfunctory
sans smoulder

music blares from raspy speakers

my white girlfriend and I watch
from a corner of the ballroom

fast forward to
my mother's question in 1996:
*who's the man and who's the woman?*

# Eat Bitterness 吃苦

You taught me that when life is hard
swallow the hurt and eat bitterness

You fled once
and 爸爸 said
I had chased you away

He brought me to
your best friend's house
and I had to beg
from the other side of the gate

Why did you return—was it
duty, love, or helplessness?

This afternoon, I am making soup
and thinking of your sacrifice

Pork ribs and bitter gourd:
eat bitterness to clear
heat from the heart

# Oceans, Unknowing

In the privacy of my thoughts, I've allowed myself to call you by your first name—Audrey, the name you chose for yourself, because you liked Audrey Hepburn.

At my desk here in Vancouver, there's a faded photograph of us in the Marine Parade flat. You, with hands in your lap, worriedly stare on while I tie the shoelaces on my red suede Pumas. Your body honed into silence. You're wearing a floral dress of pink flowers on green. It's the day of my departure from Singapore in August 1980, when I'm twenty-one, the first time that I'll be leaving you and Papa. Your shadow cast on the wall, a reminder of what's left unsaid.

More than three decades later, I've drawn closer to your absence.

*My mother did not love me.* Your voice rasps from sorrow. In the living room of your HDB flat, I am fifty-five and you, eighty. You tell me you were barely a toddler when you were shipped away to Riau to your maternal grandmother. Your father's father had insisted that you could be spared parental love and devotion, since you were not male.

Your ache is palpable, an uneasy legacy. Your hands, weathered by years of widowhood and loneliness, afraid of touching me.

Yet, it is to me that you turn, to confess your deepest sorrows. I've become the mother you yearn for. I will never succeed in disappearing that wound, no matter how hard I try. A wound that keeps resurfacing, a shadow on the wall.

Vast oceans of unknowing separate us. I've long forgiven you for failing to protect me. You dare confess, *I love you more than I love your father.*

Feeling the vastness of oceans, I have only myself to argue with in my autumnal room of solitude.

It is February 2016. Night descends on me while your morning begins. Beyond your hazy horizon is the history you've survived, distant yet present.

I abandoned the filial script, while still loving you. You might never believe me, since I won't send this letter. Or maybe it won't be words that reassure you.

# Two Tones

*for the koel bird*

I take delight in the eccentric way you sing
especially beauteous in pre-dawn quiet

Don't mind my mum's complaints
that you're noise, dispensable

If she could—she'd roast
you for dinner

In another time and place
if Hildegard von Bingen heard you sing
she might suggest there were six tones, not two

Here at the 49th parallel
in the Pacific Northwest
I summon

A memory tinged cyan
speckled cream

# Journey

*based on Six of Swords in the Tarot deck*

1.

I leave with my child
swords as protective sentinels
on either side of the vessel

The boatman's a friend
who transports us across the river
of jagged memories

If you only knew—
but then, how could you?

I've turned away from
seductive tableaux and sudden disappearances

Begun an interior journey
determined, untraceable

Rain, a misted mantle
softening my perspective
as I open to the unknown

2.

A fear of drowning
kept me enslaved for years

The comfort of familiar tropes
deceptive guise

No one talks on this crossing—
silence the chatter, to hear better

The slap of waves against the boat
the arc of swallows overhead

3.

A journey also requires
knowing what not to bring

Unspoken assumptions
that could sink me

I depend on help
to cross safely

After many days of rain
I dare hope for better weather

Truth is not promise
but compass

# Conduit

*in memory of Mariam Moussavian*

sombre clouds blanket this morning

your curiosity has departed
your voice sounding five languages
silenced

compassion was a heat
passing through you to us

in fluid syllables
you translated suffering

# In-Between

*in memory of Nancy Richler*

You entered my dream
a cold dark house with high ceilings
no furniture except chairs where
three women of colour sat, waiting

You tried to speak
but no sounds came

One of the women whispered to me,
"She doesn't know she's dead?"
I nodded, feeling sad
I hadn't been there when you passed

We had twenty-seven years as friends
reading each other's work
but in that dimmed interior with
witnesses from the underworld
we were stripped
of significance

I left you in that nowhere space
walked out onto a broad earthen road
all sunlight and expansiveness

Heading toward ceremony
dressed in bright orange-and-red robes
yet carried nothing
except my own life

# Magnetic Resonance

*for Dr. Carol Dingee*

A circle of trees congregate on the ceiling—
I don't have long to look at the Photoshop image
before the technicians slip me into the Tube

A frigid light cylinder
or time travel device

The robot bombards my body
with radio waves and magnetic fields
its thumps systematically pitched
toward some form of conclusiveness

A distant relation created this monster
that now serves or perhaps
supersedes me

I've become a ghost in the machine
as my mind
tunnels under the earth
in search of a future past

# A Lidded Jar

*in response to Edmund de Waal's exhibition "some winter pots"*

restore the tangible
for what's essential

to reverse transmute
from virtual
back to material

*

the emptiness of jars

*for food, for pulses*
*for someone's ashes*

reverential emptiness

*

sight not simply perception

if viewing on the screen
or despite of it

attention summoned
beyond

*

faded memories of life before pandemic
hibernate in the fingers
until prompted
to reach for
ephemera to satisfy
the hunger for new

*

to look to stare to wonder
at images of lidded jars

arrayed &
sealed into secrecy

their smooth surfaces
alluring dark glaze
in silent communion

gilded lead pieces
at the mouth

*

feel the imperfect
outlines of our mouths

the flaw & failure
of language

speech refracted by gild repair

\*

the lidded jar
as artefact of the imagination

the unutterable
trapped

\*

invisible
circuits
contained

until pressure & urgency
unleash
spillage
along irrational lines

\*

fear blooms into acts of violence

reduce complexities

\*

conform/contain
suppress/deflect
explode/erase

*

looming hatred
festering sorrow

shatter mouths

# Brain Wave

*for Yong Shu Hoong*

inspiration
a skin of seance
skein loosely wound
tangible if invisible

the medium appoints
a room with shifting
dimensions & textures

click ticker rhythm of fingers
on keyboard

the mind entranced
a wave a proof a visitation

# After the Storm

*for all trees*

I saw the tragedy
from my apartment window
on Sunday morning—
your huge trunk collapsed against
the tall metal barrier in the park

Today the kids from preschool
wove colourful moving dots around
your immobility

Under the light of the full moon
I went up to your fallen form

Your shallow roots exposed
next to the concrete pavement—

Gaping, textured maw

A red *Danger Do Not Enter* tape
cordoned you off as if
you're the site of a crime

Do the birds mourn your passing—
or are you crying for the children?

# Future Enterprise

Three state of the art vending booths exist in this novelty alley. Future Enterprise has become a major tourist draw, even for the locals.

*Back to Normal*, the most popular option.

Select the option, slip your $20 note into the currency sucker. Then enter the booth, sit down and hook yourself up with electrodes as shown in the demonstration video. Enjoy eight minutes of simulated normalcy. Memories are activated of former privileges such as unfettered movement, ignorance of one's impact on others. Listen to music that's sexy because it reminds you of no one else. Olfactory stimulation awakens flavours of favourite meals in restaurants, unhampered by health risks. Ignorance is bliss.

Next most popular option *Eternal Romance* floods your brain with neurotransmitters to create the experience of falling in love. Sweet scents, sex scents, scents of the sea, the illusion of an infinite horizon, accompanied by subliminal pining and sighing. Amplification of longing followed by satiation followed by longing. You pay $40 for ten minutes of exquisite torment. Any longer a duration and you're dead.

Curiously, there aren't as many people selecting the *Wealth* simulation. Perhaps the price at $50 for five minutes is too prohibitive? Even though it promises an intense experience of both *Back to Normal* and *Eternal Romance*.

A handful of humans choose *Peace* which is a steal at $10 for 20 minutes. The person gets to feel inner serenity, the opposite of excessive stimulation and attachments. Maybe humans prefer to visit sacred sites for this?

No one selects *Uncertainty*. Maybe because it's too real. We may delete this option in the next model we produce.

# That Bird Again

1.
from gut to periphery
innervations signal
an amplification of absence

shutdown/lockdown
circuit breakers
constrain

you lose muscle memory
shed visceral tone
become a shadow of your former life

2.
listening for resonance
buried beneath denials
& rhetoric

you yearn for new postures
a strategy of
innovation

3.
that bird again
in pre-dawn solo
without qualms or
hesitation
suggestive of
an imaginary possible

you recognize its voice
unseen yet
it insinuates

at times like this
human language feels
irrelevant


4.
the microscopic transgresses
boundaries

virus shapeshifts
& overrides

your psyche mutates
dissembles habits
honing an inner vision

other beings you sense
yet can't see


5.
liminal space
of micro-moment
breaths

hunger transmutes into
sustained intuiting

elsewhere
brought close

# mixed ethers

# Notes on Grieving 輓歌

*in memory of Audrey Hee, 1934-2017*

*Mummy, I'm here,*
*I'll take care of you*
I said as I entered the flat
and went to her
on the bed

she could barely move
except with the helper's assistance

*What is a healthy thing to eat?*
she asked, three days before she left

I warmed up almond milk
added some chia and flax
held the cup to her mouth

*Mae, Mae, Mae*
her voice riddled with plea and pain
several times each hour

the smell of wintergreen oil in the air
between our rooms
as the helper massaged her abdomen and back

clicking sounds of the walker
morphed to the rough whirr of the wheelchair
over seven days
she refused morphine after two doses

that last evening
in her room
upper torso slightly raised
on a rented hospital bed

I was by her side for hours
my right hand tucked under her left shoulder
my left hand on her wrist

her eyes remained wide open for an hour
then came the rattling sounds

*That's God waiting for you,* I said
*you needn't be afraid*

> I was next to her until 5.30 am
> then decided to nap on my bed
> jolted awake at 5.45 am

my mother left in those fifteen minutes
true to her habit
of escaping scrutiny

the medical doctor was delayed two hours
by traffic and rain

was she really dead
just because he said so?

             the trio of friends who came
             to pay their respects:
             Hoe Fang and Wai Han
             then Angie

their bowed heads, tears

three men arrived at 7.30 am
to wrap the corpse tightly in cloth

*swaddled* was the word that came to mind

spurts of toxic blood escaped
from her mouth
onto the sheets and the floor
as her body was moved from bed
to trolley

> I read aloud a prose poem in front of her casket
> about the girl child who
> was sent away to her maternal grandmother

the day after cremation
five of us went to Changi Pier
boarded the small boat

ocean once separated her
from her mother

we scattered ashes
she became ocean

back in the flat
the helper worried about ghosts

what was there to be afraid of?

my mum loved us


                       twin succubi
                       pressed down on my chest
                       for many nights


while in daytime, I was pale
wandering through rooms

her scent lingered
in two closets

I brushed my hand against her dresses
they whispered back

complaints against the world
bruising the cheap pages of
appointment books

ballpoint scars in a melange of
English and Chinese

her hurt sensibility
almost tearing
through

as a young mother
she was fierce tiger
ready to decimate

a rattan cane always accessible
on the kitchen wall

*spare the rod, spoil the child*

*mae si ai, bak si diah*
to scold is to love, to hit is an even greater love

*diah* being a double entendre:
love and pain entwined

years of frustrated vitality
burnt welts in my skin

        I found the appointment card
        for Polyclinic:
        she weighed in at 51.0 kg on 15/5/17
        and then 50.7 kg on 4/9/17

        a shrinking
        warrior spirit

a photograph tucked inside
my copy of *Oracle Bone*—
she's about seventy-five
the polystyrene box of rice
on the coffee table
behind her

I wonder if the delivery guy took that photo?
*Ah Swee*, she had said, *I like him a lot*

in this image, she looks serene—
her face still soft, not yet gaunt

beneath the tiger
a vulnerable soul

> was that Ah Swee I spoke to
> at the door, to tell him she was gone?

these are my notes
in which the pressure of affect
is fleeting at each appearance

unlike how her notes scarred paper
a whirlwind

my notes
an unspooling of energy
toward strangers

in a wish to transform
pain

I neither idealize nor demonize
the welts have long dissipated


     I remember her kindness
     dignified, unsentimental

     on my annual trips to Singapore
     she made sure we stopped by
     at Yong Her Sin herbal store
     to say hello

     she brewed gynostemma with fu ling
     to quell my inner heat

—Lao Gong 勞宮 Palace of Toil

how hard my loyal sentinel has been working
to shield that weakened place

the Heart which palpitates
so...so...so...so

stuttering agitated scarred
by the slightest signs
of betrayal

the needle enters
Pericardium 8 on my left palm

the earth of knowing
disappears
explodes in a rush of pain and tears

she keeps me company while I weep
*I'm sorry to cause you pain,* she says

she would have removed that needle
had I found it intolerable
but I ask for the second one
in my right palm

these weapons of liberation
shock the palace guard
with relief from duty

now I can be exhausted
enter a sleep of countless lifetimes
pinned down at the palms

she hardly hugged me
but sometimes drew close
to smell my cheek

she wasn't
held much as a child


            smell as survival instinct

she's
breathing at my cheek

sinks deeper

floats away

       still cradling her left shoulder with my right hand—
       tether feeling transmits
       phantom pain crosses

       a cyst develops on the inside of
       my left wrist at 列 缺 Lung 7
       Broken Sequence

yellowed photos potent
with patches of damp on the verso


                          tether or anchor?


not simply semantics
but about outcome

mustn't
let memories
hold me back

previous iterations of "me"—
the ones I held to be solid/independent

those selves—

I don't know
what I used to think I knew

                    so much invested in
                    the notion of certainty

                    whereas now I recognize
                    nothing ever remains the same

some days are surrendered
to floating
in-between

muffled summons
from beyond

stupor
intra-uterine liminality

no longer there but
not fully here

        our umbilical bridge conditional and conditioned
        our shared karmic tie unravels

a rash
size of my heart
a hurt heat
on my chest

pinpricks
a million forest fires

salt puts out fire
*that's why you're eating salty things*

a fire that begins unseen

*this is the nature of*
*heartbreak and anger combined*
she says, as she inserts needles
to draw out the heat

the way others avert their gaze
as if someone had just exposed their body—
you'd think there was something illicit
about how the body wears grief, or is it
the spirit roughened by loss
that's on display?

few dare to admit sadness could be sexy
or that sex might be spurred on by
the necessity not to admit grief

                    our bodies perform
                    intangible needs

                    driven by
                    anxiety of living

the unseen pull of spirit while
deaths intermingle

her father's father made that decision
to have her sent away
to her mother's mother in Riau

*My mother didn't love me*
she had wept in my arms

the sins of men
visited on daughters

a mother's love
thwarted by the will of
patriarchs

                            she pushed me away
                            with daggered insults


affection was dangerous:
being loved
being ultimately
betrayed

*Are you the man?* she had asked

she wasn't able to understand
couldn't completely accept
that I loved women

we were relegated to
each other's shadow
distant, barely perceived
until

>                her voice summoning me to dinner
>                glances and slight shifts in posture
>                the feel of sitting next to her
>                sharing food—
>
>                bright flickers
>                against darkness

at sixty
she clasped a pomelo
in front of her belly
on a street in Chinatown

pure joy
catches me by surprise


three sneezes
in the morning
announce
she's still here

that death hold
unclenches

ache dims
to a whisper

      she visits frequently in dreams—
      we plan trips

      I'm never sure
      where we're going
      but it feels good to travel together

# Flight from Memory

wings from a misspent phylogeny
vestigial & sunken
at the shoulder blades

fresh scar under the right armpit
testifies to
a minefield of deadened nerves

*

what did that side use to feel?
what did it fail to say?
or were you the one who failed to listen?

burden displaced from
a shadowy left wing

*

this is to document
what cannot be documented

\*

grief arrow
from her missed eighty-fourth year

aimed for your heart

\*

how long had that cancer been growing?

\*

to expose & question:

"sacrifice"
"duty"
"familial"

coded concepts
buried in indoctrination

\*

how did you become you?

*

evolving
that "you"

flight from fixity

no lines drawn
between before & after

*

pinion watercolours
with silvered tracings
of wings

birthed between
chemo cocktails

fastest growing cells slain
hair shed

you became a reluctant nun
laughing at death

*

do cells harmonize
deconstruct
or self-destruct

do they have choice

\*

tension between flight
& constraint

held in her arms
held back

\*

could feel & couldn't
knew yet couldn't quite

words shuttered into silence

\*

that scar still talks—
it wants you to believe
nothing else matters

\*

as if she were dying
continuously in your body

her tight, pained voice
a sacral miasma of
despair & hopelessness
clenches your throat

but look—you're alive &
more than scar
tissue

\*

hadn't you heard enough?

*too sensitive too intense*
*too angry too fussy*

*too much*

\*


a needle inserted in the right armpit—
*Heart 1 Supreme Spring*
*Utmost Source*

pinned at the apex of the fossa
where the axillary artery pulsates

a spring of qi
rushes down the arm to the hand

soft sighs
as she surfaces &
loosens her grip

*

cold colonial cruel tone

forty years on—
many still want to
pinion you to
"hard-working Chinese"
or "not one of us"

a game for many
an easy lyric

*


a concept called country
that erases the land &
genocide

violence
posing as polite & generous

I feel tainted just by being here

*

who are they—
robbed of breath
stripped of dignity?

*I can't breathe*

hatred seethes & chokes

who are they—
who pretend nothing's
the matter?

*

private life as
walled-off estate

*

escape the illusory
cage of comfort

refuse to be loyal
to loyalty itself

a rankling rawness
in place of silken pretence

\*

a wish to return
as if re-birthed
as third person
neither "you" nor "I"

beyond history & loss

\*

return to tropical heat

wings atrophied
but ready
for different trajectories

\*

cicadas telegraph heat
during an afternoon walk at
Botanic Gardens

mantle of rain
sweeps across the pond
toward you

*

I read that
children wear wings in a Taiyuan school
in Shanxi province
to maintain social distancing

*


we are beginning to mutate

can you feel it?

*


on the green field below:
two children in raincoats
bright yellow specks
contrast with two adults in dark clothing

a Yayoi vibration
pulsating networks

while the observer "I"
is a nexus

a pop-up operation
here to witness
new life

\*

mother, mater, matter

stripped of
romantic aspiration

a conundrum—

to document what cannot
be documented

from time to new

# Returned

*in memory of Ryuichi Sakamoto*

The first thing we see
is the inside of a piano
the flashlight points while
the voice comments

*as if playing the corpse of the piano
that had drowned*

He strokes the beast's flank
sits down and starts to play
the life
tuned by a tsunami

# Lost

She's forgotten her way back

trying one elevator then another
every floor, unfamiliar

the concrete tower
surprises with
a mid-level indoor swimming pool
while there's a security guard and CCTV
in the basement

She waits there
while I search on her behalf

Waking up, I'm still somewhat disoriented

She's been lost
for several years
but I now sense a way
to bring her home

# The Stranger

the pigeon across the street flies
into the side of a moving car
lands on the ground
dazed

I am too far away to help
in a blink she disappears

I wince from the realization
that each moment
contains
innumerable disappearances
unseen by anyone

# Sipping Tea

A gift of pu'er tea leaves
in a global pandemic

To taste earthiness
maturation as pleasure

Leaves from ancient trees
in Yunnan province
aged until
the dark liquor yields
sombre companionship

Privation and privilege

No matter how reclusive
I depend on the efforts of others

# Impossible Proposition

wind whistles
through interstices

I observe charisma
unconvinced

veils are flimsy

seal of veracity
an illusion

this *now* that flees into

# Myth

innumerable
silences
shadowed
metaphors

you tell me I'm not lonely
you tell me who I am

once a
peach-faced lovebird
good at chattering & entertaining
my true form camouflaged

by cascade of noise &
bullying presumptions

wearied & wary
of the cage
I've flown

to a distant utopia
where a large bell sounds out
across the wide span of silence
to herald
a crossing

this too is a myth

# Reflections On Refuge
*based on a visit to Enoura Observatory, Odawara, Japan*

You sit on murmurs or sink your vision into Sagami Bay beyond. Fossils nestle next to a bamboo grove. Smooth gleam of two modern sculptures confess the impossibility of precision, helpless in the midst of faded Buddha statuary. Enshrined in glass, a stone rod—from a time when sekken were meant to draw the kami down, long before the sword was shaped for battle. Trust in the tunnels that lead you away or toward— walk through time or wait for the ending of it. While crossing this bridge of floating quarry stones, you realize that resolve is required. Here and there, a tomeishi arrests your movement, reminds you the architect is speaking. On this afternoon of quadruple 2s, pause to consider the limits of human nature.

\*

*I owe a lot to Odawara. For one thing, my earliest childhood memory is of the sea seen from the window of the Shonan train, running on the old Tokaido line from Atami to Odawara. When we came out of the twin tunnels, there was the vast Pacific, extending away to a sharp horizon line that snapped my eyes wide open. In that moment I also awoke to the fact that I was me, and that I was here on this earth.*

— Hiroshi Sugimoto, architect and visionary

As he described it, that precise moment seemed like a singular perception; and yet, it was the culmination of innumerable, untraceable moments. Perhaps emerging from the dark tunnel, the horizon line functioned like the visual equivalent of a Zen master's kyōsaku, thwacking the dulled mind into an awakening.

An awareness of infinity based on the realization of constraint? Either one fights against this truth or decides to be humbled and inspired.

*

We enter light after passing through tunnels. We stumble into a time of conjunctions. An ephemeral glimpse.

*

A support stone from the original Moon Crossing-Bridge in Arashiyama now rests here. It languished on the riverbed until recognized, hole at a diagonal, the place where it used to support one of the angled legs of the bridge.

A wound in time, a displaced function.

You too had been fashioned to hold others up.

*

You are transitioning toward uselessness. Refusing to function according to script. Once, your youthful ego preferred hard edges. Worn down with time, having travelled through several tunnels of transition, you are disoriented and apprehensive, waiting for that moment your life must change yet again.

*

On August 6, 1945, when the atom bomb was dropped, the pagoda roof close to Ground Zero was instantly pulverized from thermal rays and radiation. Now nestled in the bamboo grove at Enoura, it hums with the echo of its destruction.

Place being no guarantee of refuge, subject to constant movement. Refuge being endlessly redefined, and we along with it.

*

Stones from Nebukawa quarry nearby have been transformed into smooth, flat surfaces that hover just above ground. You cross this floating bridge a second time, from time's shore to uncertainty.

# Eating Laksa

1.

in situ or
in neuronal

taste fleeting

synaptic wings

from time to
new

2.

days of Glory
on East Coast Road

steaming cauldron of
laksa broth
induces
an olfactory hypnosis

3.

at the corner kopitiam on Ceylon Road

fifty years after wearing Haig Girls' uniforms
Soh Kiak & I meet to eat laksa

4.

*the original Katong laksa*

laksa, victim of
false claims

death defiance
immortality &
spice eugenics


5.

what is original?
what is pure?


6.

lakhshah in Hindi
lakshas in Sanskrit

language slurps
elusive noodles

7.

global hype of
a hybrid shape-shifter

laksa's diasporic
drift

I pull a packet off
the shelf at T&T

the taste is never the same
but close


8.

I do not yearn for the past
but feel its absence
between tongue & teeth

# Three Chinese Aunties

Two flights of steps
above the community garden
the neo-Daoist pantheon
presides over their Vancouver specials

A pair of Immortals work from low stools
to water lush giant lettuce
in adjacent plots
while conversing in Toisanese

Although unschooled in divine speech
I offer a compliment, 好大 hou dai

A snow-haired sprite
dances along the sidewalk
keeps an eye on the grandkids
playing hockey in the front yard

Several homes display the same indigo sign—
"This is OUR HOME
這是我們的家
development without displacement"

The pantheon must have won—
lettuce, the only monsters thriving

# One Chicken Rice Recalls Another

the way she relished the sauces—
ginger, chilli, dark soy

here, thousands of miles away
the chicken rice from Cafe D'Lite
meets Southeast Asian
hawker standard

a taste that activates memory

that past life distanced
yet my belly recalls her

# Turning

*for H.*

when you feel the past
is a stranger

search for history yet
it's now faint trace

they say it's a corner
but the turning was sinuous

an altered consciousness
emerges from the labyrinth
tracks how twists trapped

now that you aren't there
you trust
propulsion

# Walking, As If

stitching
a map

as if still in childhood
watching the roti prata man
corner of Koon Seng and Joo Chiat

his deft slap of dough on the oily surface
extends large then largest
arrives sizzling on the plate

or—further down the street
caramelized hints of rock sugar
wafting from the confectionary

we grew up in the same neighbourhood
a decade apart

we have walked together
only a few times
separated by trajectory

that Joo Chiat—when our mothers
were still alive—
no longer exists

how then to piece together
a shared tapestry
to settle a debt
to place?

# Block 17

an address for more than four decades
a home that wasn't

I look up at fifteenth-floor windows
portal to my room

minus the metal grills
that had kept me from jumping

a retired couple now live where
my mother spent lonely years

six years of her absence
a whole lifetime left behind

the breeze swirls
around my body of difference

# Shards

*written in response to an art show featuring art by Naoko Fukumaru*

1.

that nothing survives whole
!
!
!
that breakage is not the end of beauty
((                    ))
^^ {}                    [ ]

that there are infinite possibilities
but finite opportunities

a golden seam

2.

I am a circle of broken pieces
rearranged to form a visual puzzle
gaps between shards

3.

the fiction of stitching
the stitching of fiction

# Get Into Yourself: a found poem
*for Jay Sensei*

belly to thigh             feel the stretch

don't hurt yourself though

                    yeah, that's it

six slow breaths                  beautiful

one hand behind you & twist to the back

Taikokyu 體呼吸          your body breathing

feet together in Water Stretch
forearms on the floor
lower yourself down
chin toward body

                         move your core
                         don't hurt yourself though

six
          slow
                    breaths

in through your nose
out through your mouth

                    don't bounce, but deepen with your breath

          yeah, that's it

good work

                    beautiful

# Tender

today, on Qing Ming
they sweep away
the unhoused in DTES
as if clearing the tombs of ancestors
of vermin

antithesis of reverence—
pissing on pain
self-righteous violence

but wait, just wait

the ancestors aren't
confined to one day

bones of the earth
flee into
the hearts of flowers

burst forth, living & dying
in perpetuity

restlessly
seeking
a pulsing warmth

a flowering heart

# Sniffing Butts

several labradoodles, one boxer
INFP speckled heeler
uppity pomeranian
a laid-back chow chow

running joyously
sniffing butts

some into polyamorous partying
whereas the pomeranian prefers to terrify
the bigger but meeker dog

others are loners who need lots of time out
at the water fountain
or else—torn between staying hydrated or
losing themselves in revelry

outside the enclosure
I'm thinking of a bygone era

no more sniffing
or kissing ass
for me

# A Monster Dreams

at first, the familiar depiction looms
over the Tokyo landscape
all set to terrorize and destroy

it's a dream of a fiction
twentieth-century apocalyptic narrative

I understand this well
so why does it change?

sheds its hide from tough scaly
to a pliable skin of chartreuse and mauve
wears plum lipstick and smiles

poised to step into
a different genre

# Being Human
*for* 劉太

in the open pavilion at Aberdeen Park
watching her move
I disappear

her Taiji moves show
decades of practice and skill

quiet confidence outside
of social media presence

having chased after appearances
and fame all these years
I'm now willing to
surrender

she's in her seventies
spirit and body strong

offers me a chance
to practice together

I look up at the sky
reminded
of impermanence

# Rose Angels

*in memory of Harold Budd*

pink rose
crystal sparkling

angels with walking canes
wee ones in diapers

those whose lust
frays their uniforms

father playing soccer
with daughter in hijab

elderly aunties gossip
line dance on the baseball diamond

toddlers pant
interminably surmounting slides

polyvalent linguistic wings
that twirl and lift and fly

in this bright, liminal
shadowed present

a madrigal on
infinite loop

# & Found

& now you've followed me here to this eleventh-floor
home in Renfrew-Collingwood

no view of the ocean but perhaps the gigantic neon cross
on top of the Catholic church comforts you

gradually at ease in the strongly Asian neighbourhood
even tempted to join the seniors practising qigong

you're finding your way through the area
stopping to admire the vegetable gardens

familiar with being dwarfed by tall buildings
your eyes sparkle with anticipation at the blackberry bushes
behind the community garden

pleased there aren't the noisy koel birds of Marine Terrace
but not minding the squadrons of seagulls & crows
in Gaston Park

do you like that photo of us taken on your eightieth birthday
that now sits next to grandma's Peranakan belt?

I hear you say *eat fish every day*
mollified by my high dose fish oil capsules

you complain how dusty it gets
but at least I always have food in the fridge

Mummy, the memories fade
but here
you&I together

# notes

The quote in the epigraph is from the poem "A Wild Patience Has Taken Me This Far" by Mary Jean Chan in her book titled *Flèche* (London: Faber & Faber, 2019). Used with permission from the author.

**distant shore**

Cloudscapes parts 1 and 2 appeared online in *the pi review of poetry*, September 2020.

An earlier version of "Digging for Clams" was published in *Voice & Verse Poetry Magazine*, Issue 56 on the theme "Home."

"Eat Bitterness, 吃苦" was published in Issue 45.2 (Tipping Point) of *Room Magazine*.

An earlier version of "Oceans, Unknowing" appeared in *PRESS: 100 Love Letters*, edited by Laurel Flores Fantauzzo and Francesca Rendle-Short (Diliman: University of the Philippines Press, 2017).

"Journey" appeared in *No News*, edited by Paul Munden, Alvin Pang and Shane Strange (Canberra: No Work Press, 2020)

"Magnetic Resonance" appeared in *Voice & Verse Poetry Magazine*, 2018, Issue 44 themed "1818."

"A Lidded Jar" was written in response to a virtual viewing of Edmund de Waal's exhibition "some winter pots" at Gagosian Gallery (from December 3, 2020 to January 16, 2021).

"After the Storm" appeared in *Voice & Verse Poetry Magazine*, 2023, Issue 70 themed "Neighbourhood."

An earlier version of "Future Enterprise" appeared online at poetrycanada.org.

**mixed ethers**

輓歌 wǎngē means "elegy" in Chinese.

An excerpt from "Notes on Grieving" appeared in *Canadian Literature*, Issue 236, Spring 2018.

Excerpts from "Notes on Grieving" and "Flight from Memory" appeared in *Atelier of Healing*, an online anthology, edited by Eric Valles and Desmond Kon, 2021.

Excerpts from "Flight from Memory" were featured online in *the pi review of poetry*, September 2020.

The line "I can't breathe" was what George Floyd said as Derek Chauvin the police officer knelt on his neck before being killed by Chauvin on May 25th, 2020.

**from time to new**

"Returned" refers to a scene in *Coda*, a 2018 documentary film made by Stephen Nomura Schible about Ryuichi Sakamoto.

"Impossible "Proposition" first appeared online in *the pi review of poetry* in September 2020 titled as "Vulnerability." It is now featured on poetrycanada.org.

"Reflections on Refuge" is based on an afternoon visit to Enoura Observatory in Odawara, Japan on February 20, 2020. The quote by Hiroshi Sugimoto was taken from the website for Enoura Observatory: https://www.odawara-af.com/en/enoura/.

Some excerpts from "Eating Laksa" appeared online in *the pi review of poetry*, September 2020.

The whole poem sequence "Eating Laksa" appeared in the ASIA issue of *Rabbit*. Issue 33.

"Three Aunties" was first published in Issue 45.2 (Tipping Point) of *Room Magazine*.

"Shards" was written in response to an art show featuring Kintsugi art by Naoko Fukumaru, at Richmond Art Gallery, July-August 2021.

An earlier version of "Walking, As If" appears online at poetrycanada. org.

"Rose Angels" is dedicated to Harold Budd, an ambient/avant-garde music composer who died from COVID in 2020; the poem makes allusions to "Madrigals of the Rose Angel" composed in 1972. It appeared in *Voice & Verse Poetry Magazine*, 2023, Issue 70 themed "Neighbourhood."

# Acknowledgements

The idea for this book began with attempts to write two long poems; first, about my mother's cancer and dying; next, in response to receiving a diagnosis of breast cancer nine months after my mum's passing. Both long poems are in the middle section, and all else grew, like a blossoming spiral, from this centre. Much gratitude and appreciation to all the friends and healthcare professionals who supported my mother and me through those hard times.

Many of these poems pay tribute to my mother's life and her continuation in me; other poems are dedicated to friends or creative/spiritual influences, some no longer alive but still felt. In particular, Thich Nhat Hanh's teachings on impermanence and continuation were very much present in my mind as I worked on this manuscript. There were countless others—strangers, both human and non-human—whose very existence inspired me. My hope is that this book will not only speak to other poets and writers, but also to those whose lives have been affected by loss or illness.

Thank you, The Poecupine's Quill, for believing in this book. Deep appreciation to Shane Neilson for the careful editorial guidance, and to Jeremy Luke Hill for the design of the book and cover. Thanks to Mary Jean Chan, for permission to quote a line from her poem.

Appreciation to the various print and online magazines and anthologies that published earlier versions of some poems. Thanks to Cathy Stonehouse who provided feedback on some poems; to Sweden Xiao for the Chinese term 晚歌 which means "elegy." My profound gratitude to Yong Shu Hoong whose insightful comments and suggestions went a very long way toward the realization of this manuscript.

# About the Author

Lydia Kwa has lived and worked on the traditional and unceded territories of the Coast Salish peoples since 1992. She is a psychologist in private practice as well as a writer.

Kwa has previously published two books of poetry (*The Colours of Heroines*, 1994; *sinuous*, 2013) and five novels (*This Place Called Absence*, 2000; *The Walking Boy*, 2005 and 2019; *Pulse*, 2010 and 2014; *Oracle Bone*, 2017; *A Dream Wants Waking*, 2023).

She won the 2018 Earle Birney Poetry Prize for best poem published in *PRISM international*.

Her novels have been nominated for several awards, including the Lambda Literary Award for Fiction.

Kwa has exhibited her art work at Centre A (2014) and Massy Art Gallery (2018) and has self-published two poetry-visual art chapbooks.